WHAT'S THE DIFFERENCE?
SUMMER AND WINTER
SPRING AND AUTUMN

Heather Amery
Illustrated by Peter Firmin

Consultant: Betty Root
Centre for the Teaching of Reading
University of Reading, England

Spring in the country

The birds are building their nest. The farmer is ploughing his fields.

Autumn in the country

The birds are getting ready to fly away for the winter.
It is harvest time for the farmer.

Spring in the garden

There is lots of planting to do.
The baby is in his pram.

Autumn in the garden

Now there is lots of fruit to pick.
Where is the baby?

Spring in the garden

The children have a garden of their own.
What do you think they are doing?

Autumn in the garden

Now you can see what they have grown.
How many vegetables can you count?

Spring in the park

There are new leaves on the tree.
How many ducklings can you see?

Autumn in the park

The leaves are falling off the trees.
What has happened to the ducklings?

Spring by the pond

There are lots of tadpoles in the pond.
The swan is sitting on her nest.

Autumn by the pond

The reeds have grown tall and thick.
How many frogs can you see?

Summer by the sea

It is hot and sunny on the beach. What are all the children doing?

Winter by the sea

It is cold and windy on the beach. What are these children doing?

Summer in the garden

The children like playing with the hose,
and having tea in the garden.

Winter in the garden

The birds are hungry.
What is the dog doing?

Summer in the garden

It is very hot and dry.
The flowers need lots of water.

Winter in the garden

The garden is cold and wet.
But there are still things to play with.

Summer in the park

It is fun playing in the park in summer.
How many children are eating icecream?

Winter in the park.

It is fun playing in the winter too.
What are the ducks doing?

Summer by the pond

It is cool playing in the water.
How many ducks can you count?

Winter by the pond.

The pond is frozen now.
What are all the birds doing?

Summer in the street

The town is hot and dry. Everyone is wearing their summer clothes.

Winter in the street.

he town is cold and wet. What are all the children doing?

Puzzle picture

Would you see these things in spring, summer, autumn or winter?

First published in 1985. Usborne Publishing Ltd, 20 Garrick Street, London WC2E 9BJ, England. ©Usborne Publishing Ltd. 1985

The name Usborne and the device 🐝 are Trade Marks of Usborne Publishing Ltd.

Printed in Portugal.